YOUR KNOWLEDGE H

- We will publish your bachelor's and
  master's thesis, essays and papers

- Your own eBook and book -
  sold worldwide in all relevant shops

- Earn money with each sale

Upload your text at www.GRIN.com
and publish for free

Bibliographic information published by the German National Library:

The German National Library lists this publication in the National Bibliography; detailed bibliographic data are available on the Internet at http://dnb.dnb.de .

Imprint:

Copyright © 2017 GRIN Verlag, Open Publishing GmbH
Print and binding: Books on Demand GmbH, Norderstedt Germany
ISBN: 9783668594944

This book at GRIN:

https://www.grin.com/document/383480

Carolin Peters

Aus der Reihe: e-fellows.net stipendiaten-wissen

e-fellows.net (Hrsg.)

Band 2636

Consequences of the Sarbanes-Oxley Act. Financial Accounting and Reporting Quality, Capital Market

GRIN Publishing

GRIN - Your knowledge has value

Since its foundation in 1998, GRIN has specialized in publishing academic texts by students, college teachers and other academics as e-book and printed book. The website www.grin.com is an ideal platform for presenting term papers, final papers, scientific essays, dissertations and specialist books.

Visit us on the internet:

http://www.grin.com/

http://www.facebook.com/grincom

http://www.twitter.com/grin_com

Universität Potsdam

Wirtschafts- und Sozialwissenschaftliche Fakultät

Lehrstuhl für Rechnungswesen und Wirtschaftsprüfung
im privaten und öffentlichen Sektor

Seminararbeit

zum Thema
„Consequences of the Sarbanes-Oxley Act"
im Rahmen des Forschungsseminars
„Current Issues in Accounting and Auditing"
Sommersemester 2017

Eingereicht von:

Peters, Carolin

Potsdam, den 30.04.2017

Table of Contents

I

List of Abbreviations

AS	Auditing Standard
ASK	Ashbaugh-Skaife
EM	earnings management
ICD	internal control deficiencies
ICW	internal control weaknesses
MWD	material weakness disclosure
PCAOB	Public Company Accounting Oversight Board
SEC	Securities and Exchange Commission
SOX	Sarbanes-Oxley Act
SOX 302	Section 302 of the Sarbanes-Oxley Act
SOX 404	Section 404 of the Sarbanes-Oxley Act

1 Introduction

The Sarbanes-Oxley Act (SOX) was introduced by President George W. Bush in the year 2002 (cf. Beneish et al., 2008, p. 669). This regulation changed disclosure and reporting requirements (Leuz and Wysocki, 2016, p. 526) and aims to increase trust of the investors in capital markets again, after facing several balance and accounting scandals between the years 2000 and 2002, for example at Enron and WorldCom (cf. Hogan and Wilkins, 2008, p. 222). The SOX affects companies with a registration at the Securities and Exchange Commission (SEC) (cf. Beneish et al., 2008, p. 666). There are two sections that are considered having a high impact on the corporate governance of complying firms, Section 302 (SOX 302) and Section 404 (SOX 404) (cf. Zhang, 2007, pp. 82-83). SOX 302 - "Corporate Responsibility for Financial Reports"- demands the executives to assess whether firms' financial statements represent the financial situation and the results of the operations and the period. Executives should design, establish and maintain internal controls. An evaluation of the effectiveness, disclosures of deficiencies concerning internal controls, frauds et cetera is necessary (SOX, 2002, Section 302). SOX 404 - "Management Assessment of Internal Controls"- extends prior requirements and demands that the company's external auditor must report on the reliability of management's assessment of internal control every fiscal year. It also requires an annual attestation by the management that evaluates the reliability of financial statements (SOX, 2002, Section 404). Especially SOX 404 is considered a cost driver of the SOX and demands significant changes in financial reporting. Aim of SOX 302 and 404 is to improve internal controls, and to reduce opportunistic behaviour of executives (cf. Zhang, 2007, pp. 82-83).

Prior studies show evidence that there seem to be differences between the perceived benefits and the target effects of the SOX, for example regarding audit quality after the SOX (cf. DeFond and Zhang, 2014, p.312). Furthermore, there is a discussion questioning whether the SOX can be characterized as symbolic politics, or as an effective regulatory intervention (cf. Romano, 2005, pp. 1585-1586). Hence, to evaluate the consequences and effectiveness of the SOX, there will be a focus on the impact of the sections that are considered having a high impact on complying firms. Therefore, a literature review will be made. The chapter "Conceptual Background" provides additional information about the SOX and describes different factors that can be regarded to assess the SOX. In "Empirical Findings", prior studies that evaluate these factors will be considered, compared and allocated to two categories: "Financial Accounting and Reporting Quality" and "Capital Market Consequences". The first includes factors like audit quality, earnings quality, and therefore the reliability and accuracy of financial statements. Latter describes investor's reactions after the introduction of the SOX. At the end, a conclusion about the consequences and the effectiveness of the SOX will be drawn.

2 Conceptual Background

Before the SOX, auditing was a self-regulating industry that was overseen by a government agency which was the U.S. Securities and Exchange Commission (SEC). A quasi-governmental agency, the Public Company Accounting Oversight Board (PCAOB), is responsible for controlling the industry since introduction of the SOX (cf. DeFond and Francis, 2005, p. 6). The SOX of 2002 aims "to protect investors by improving the accuracy and reliability of corporate disclosures made pursuant to the securities laws, and for other purposes" (SOX, 2002, 116 stat.745). Although there may be perceived benefits, regulatory intervention is considered being costly (cf. DeFond and Zhang, 2014, p. 304). The question is whether this regulatory intervention improves accounting, reporting and audit quality or not, and how investors assess that. Especially latter describes the perceived effects of the SOX.

Stock prices and cost of capital are possible indicators for the effectiveness and have been evaluated in prior studies. They show whether investor's trust in financial statements increased or not (cf. Beneish, 2008, p. 666). There is also the possibility to evaluate the quality of accounting and financial reporting directly. Regarding this, it might be useful to assess the extent and the development of earnings management (EM) which can either be accrual-based or based on real activities (cf. Cohen et al., 2008, p. 762). Due to imposed assessment of financial statements by external auditors, the influence on audit quality will be evaluated, too. SOX 302 became effective on August 29, 2002 (cf. Raghunandan and Rama, 2006, p. 110). It is important to distinguish between accelerated filers and non-accelerated filers. Accelerated filers are firms that had a market-capitalization of at least $ 75 million by the end of the year 2002. For these firms, SOX 404 became mandatory for fiscal years ending after November 15, 2004 (cf. Beneish et al., 2008, p. 668). Hence, prior internal control deficiencies (ICD) disclosures were voluntary for firms. For foreign registrants and non-accelerated filers, SOX 404 is effective for fiscal year-ends on or after July 15, 2007 (cf. Raghunandan and Rama, 2006, pp. 100-101). Regarding the characteristics of the internal control weaknesses (ICW), three different categories can be made. The first is "material weaknesses", the second is "control deficiencies" and the third one is "significant deficiencies". Material weaknesses may lead to a material misstatement and significant deficiencies might lead to possible misstatements, which are less severe than material misstatements. It is important to notice that the auditor must issue an adverse opinion on internal controls, in case not identified material weaknesses exist after the firm's compliance with SOX 404 (PCAOB 2004, AS No. 2, §§8-10 & §129).

"Higher quality earnings provide more information about the features of a firm's financial performance that are relevant to a specific decision made by a specific decision-maker." (Dechow et al., 2010, p. 344) The relevance of underlying financial performance to decisions and the ability of an accounting system to measure performance has an impact on earnings quality (cf. Dechow et al., 2010, p. 344). Earnings quality can be measured with various proxies, for example "persistence" which means that firms have more sustainable earnings or cash flows. The magnitude of accruals indicates a less persistent component of earnings, if extreme accruals are observable. Smoothness can be influenced through managers who attempt to smooth repeating changes in cash flows (volatility). Consequently, earnings quality suffers from a less timely and less informative earnings number. A timely loss recognition stands for higher earnings quality because it mitigates management's natural optimism. "Investor responsiveness" means that investors respond to information with value implications. Other external indicators, for example an ICD report, means that this specific firm had errors or are likely to have had an error (ICD disclosure) in their financial reporting system. This is an indicator for low quality earnings (cf. Dechow et al., 2010, pp. 351-352).

EM influences earnings quality and can either be accrual-based or based on real activities (e.g. investment activities or reduction of research & development costs). A possible aim of these manipulations is to meet certain earning targets. Managers might trade off these EM methods or might reduce manipulation due to the new requirements of the SOX (cf. Zang, 2012, pp. 676 – 781). There are different incentives for executives to manage earnings, for example bonus grants and option-based compensations. Due to that, they choose different accounting methods (cf. Cohen et al., 2008, pp. 759-761). SOX 302 and 404 mandate the return of any incentive compensation and their requirement which may lead to a less opportunistic behavior of the executives, if the SOX is effective (cf. Cohen et al.,

2008, pp. 780-781). Accrual-based EM primarily focuses on changing accounting methods or estimates used accounting methods when illustrating the transactions in financial statements (cf. Zang, 2012, p. 676). The magnitude of accruals influences the net income of each firm. Better internal control helps to gain more realistic and reliable figures and helps to conduct information about production, sales, management of inventory, the financial situation et cetera. Executives might not be able to specify a reliable magnitude of accruals in case of weak internal controls, so unintentional misstatements are possible due to inappropriate internal controls. This leads to noisier and less reliable financial information. Unintentional misstatements can occur because of a lack of adequate policies, training or diligence by firm employees. Intentional misstatements are possible, too. In addition, it is easier for managers or employees with weak internal controls to create biased accruals to meet their opportunistic financial reporting goals or to steal. If accrual manipulation decreases, this might indicate positive effects of the SOX (cf. ASK et al., 2008, pp. 221-222).

Roychowdhury defines real activities manipulation as "departures from normal operational practices, motivated by managers' desire to mislead at least some stakeholders into believing certain financial reporting goals have been met in the normal course of operations" (Roychowdhury, 2006, p. 337). In contrast to accruals-based manipulation, it is not possible to manipulate through real activities at the end of the year. Instead of that, manipulations during the fiscal year are possible (cf. Zang, 2012, p. 681). Sales manipulation, overproduction or the reduction of discretionary expenses are possible ways to influence operational activities. It is possible that real activities reduce firm value, for example because price discounts lead to costumer expectations that price discounts exist in future periods, too. Hence, short-term benefits like meeting a certain earning target can be reached, but it can lead to a decrease in cash flows in future periods due to lower margins (cf. Roychowdhury, 2006, pp. 337-341). A decrease in accrual-based EM might occur after the SOX because this manipulation method is easier to detect (cf. Cohen et al., 2008, p. 772) and managers want to avoid penalties. Other reasons are the adverse publicity and the oncoming legal costs for executives and firms that were accused of fraudulent or questionable reporting practices (cf. Cohen et al., 2008, pp. 761-765).

Higher audit quality can be defined as "greater assurance that the financial statements faithfully reflect the firm's underlying economics, conditioned on its financial reporting system and innate characteristics" (DeFond and Zhang, 2014, p. 276). This illustrates that higher audit quality has a positive impact on the quality of financial statements and improves financial reporting quality. If the credibility of the financial reports is high, it has a positive impact on financial reporting quality (cf. DeFond and Zhang, 2014, p. 276). Smaller and less profitable firms might be more likely to experience ICD because their lack of resources to implement a working operating- and information-system. Audit quality, and therefore the choice of audit firms, may also have an impact on the likeliness to disclose ICD. Firms with prior restatements might be more likely to detect ICD because they had less sophisticated financial information before. Firms with a high concentration of institutional shareholders are predicted to be more likely to report ICD under voluntary SOX 302 disclosures because they demand changes. New managers may be more likely to detect and report ICD because they can blame other parties, for example the ex-CEO, for that. Firms might also be more likely to detect and report ICD when they have recently dismissed their auditor. In that case, executives are expected to improve their financial reporting system due to the possibility to blame the recent dismissed auditor for existing ICD (cf. ASK et al., 2007, pp. 172-175).

Weaknesses cause additional work for the disclosing firm itself and the auditing firm, for example because of changes and testing in the audit program. Higher audit fees may be an indicator for better audit quality. Material weaknesses can cause a rise in the risk premium of an auditor which leads to higher audit fees due to possible present accounting issues, too (cf. Raghunandan and Rama, 2006, p. 102). ICD disclosures might lead to a significant stock price reaction. Investors reevaluate their prior assessment of the financial reporting, the quality of the accounting system and the quality of the management's oversight over financial reporting. This has an impact on the expectations of the investors concerning future cash flows of the firms and the risk. Some of the information resulting from ICW disclosures are used by the investors with the aim to overthink their expectations regarding the firm value (cf. Lambert et al., 2007, pp. 394-395). Stock price reactions to critical events surrounding SOX (for example its introduction) might occur and the question is whether such stock price effects are influenced by the extent firms had managed their earnings. If the SOX is effective, it mitigates information uncertainty for investors due to more reliable and accurate financial statements. The SOX is also expected to reduce agency costs which increases shareholder wealth and to impose higher cost of capital on firms with prior extensive EM activities (cf. Li et al., 2008, pp. 112-113).

Accelerated filers need to have independently audited internal controls after SOX 404 is effective, and may operate in a more informative environment than non-accelerated filers that are often associated with a smaller firm size and poorer financial reporting quality. Thus, material weakness disclosures made under SOX 302 might have a higher impact on non-accelerated filers due to a higher information content for investors. Hence, material weakness disclosures are expected to affect stock prices of material weakness firms making a disclosure under SOX 302 negatively because investors expect future cash flows to be more uncertain (cf. Beneish et al., 2008, pp. 668-674). There might be effects of the SOX on the opacity of firms and relation between the transparency of financial statements and the distribution of stock returns. Due to the SOX and the resulting consequences (e.g. increased penalties for earnings manipulation), SOX effectiveness would result in greater model error (R^2) of the Jones Modell (cf. Jones, 1991) which estimates non-discretionary accrual components and less intentional accruals management which is used as a direct and firm-specific measure of opacity. Hence, opacity for idiosyncratic and crash risk might decline in post-SOX times due to new regulatory environment. In this environment, firms can hide less information (cf. Hutton et al., 2009, p. 84).

Returns are an indicator of all public information. They are important for investors to assess possible investments. If an earnings number is realistic, information risk decreases (cf. Francis et al., 2004, p. 974). Regarding the principal-agent theory and the information asymmetry between manager and investors, this can result in moral hazard and adverse selection that can influence the efficiency of investments (cf. Cheng et al., 2013, p. 4). When moral hazard occurs, managers follow other aims than investors and try to influence investor's decisions, for example when they overrate revenues for a segment they would like to expand. This may lead to an over-investment of ICD firms that do not face financial constraints. With a disclosure of ICW, it is possible to mitigate these problems and to increase the quality of financial information and therefore the efficiency of investments (cf. Cheng et al., 2013, pp. 3-4).

3 Empirical Findings

In this chapter, there will be a distinction between the effects of the SOX for financial accounting and reporting quality and for the capital markets. In some cases, an assignment to both areas may be possible because studies examine both. There will be a classification based on the area where consequences mainly occur. As described before, there will be a focus on SOX 302 and 404 that are considered having a high impact on complying firms regarding their internal controls.

3.1 Financial Accounting and Reporting Quality

There is evidence that managers tend to avoid reporting losses manipulating real activities. In firms with debt outstanding and a higher market-to-book ratio, managers tend to manipulate through real activities. Managers, especially those working for firms reporting small positive profits and small positive forecast errors, use real activities manipulation is to avoid negative annual forecast errors (cf. Roychowdhury, 2006, pp. 359-365). Zang uses a sample of more than 6.500 EM suspect firm years over the period 1987-2008 and with regression analyses for each industry year (cf. Zang, 2012, p. 687), she shows that institutional investors seem to impose more constraint and scrutiny over real activities manipulation due to longer-term real consequences on firm values. There are factors that constraint accrual-based management which are the presence of high-quality auditors on the one hand, and increased scrutiny of accounting practice since the introduction of the SOX on the other hand. She finds evidence that managers trade off the two strategies depending on their relative costliness of the approaches. Using Hausman test (cf. Hausman, 1978), she documents that real activities manipulation precedes accrual-based EM. Managers tend to "fine-tune" accruals after the fiscal-year end, depending on the extent of prior real activity manipulation, which implies the existence of two different timing strategies. She finds that a substitution of the approaches occurs (cf. Zang, 2012, pp. 698-700). This is quite consistent with the following results.

Cohen, Dey and Lys investigate the extent of real EM and accrual-based EM in prior- and post-SOX times. They divide their sample into different subsamples to compare the different periods, prior- and post-SOX period (1987-2001 and 2002-2005) (cf. Cohen et al., 2008, p. 762). They use cash flow data and the modified Jones model (cf. Dechow et al., 1995) to estimate firm-specific normal accruals for their sample firms. To evaluate the level of real activities EM, they consider the abnormal levels of cash flow from operations, discretionary expenses and production costs (cf. Cohen et al., 2008, pp. 762-765). They find increasing accrual-based EM in prior-SOX times which reached a peak in the years when the highly publicized accounting scandals occurred (2000 and 2001). During that time, they find a decline in real EM and that the relevance of income-increasing EM rises. In contrast to that, the relevance of income-decreasing EM goes down. Accrual-based EM decreases over the sample period and especially after the introduction of the

SOX and additionally, overall level of EM increased. After controlling for compensation structure, the authors are not able to detect higher accrual-based EM activities in the years during the scandals. In contrast, they find higher real earnings activities in the year 2000 - 2001. They find evidence for an association between the increase in accrual-based EM and an increase in option-based compensation, especially in the scandal period. In post-SOX times, there is a significant decline in this relation and option-based compensation decreases as well. These findings imply that executives changed their EM technique and focused on real activities management in the post-SOX period due to the difficulty to detect this technique, although this method is costlier. The authors examine the different EM activities of firms that have shown a likeliness to manage their earnings before, and find evidence that these firms had significantly higher discretionary accruals in prior-SOX and post-SOX times. After the SOX, a decrease in accrual-based EM and an increase in real activities EM occurred among those firms (cf. Cohen et al., 2008, pp. 777-783).

Ashbaugh-Skaife (ASK), Collins, Kinney and LaFond use data from accelerated filers that disclosed ICD under SOX 302 and compared managements' prior SOX opinions with external audit reports made under SOX 404 to estimate the influence of ICD on the quality of reported accruals with cross-sectional tests (cf. ASK et al., 2008, p. 228). They show that firms with ICD disclosures showed larger absolute, larger positive accruals relative to firms without ICD. They also show that firms exhibiting ICW have larger negative abnormal total and abnormal working capital accruals relative to firms without an ICD (cf. ASK et al., 2008, p. 233). A decrease in absolute abnormal accruals can be recognized in the first post-SOX 404 year after first reporting ICD. ICD firms with an opponent opinion following SOX 404 show no significant change in the magnitude of their abnormal accruals. Those firms that improved internal controls in the post SOX 404 year, seem to achieve a modest increase in accrual quality. In contrast to that, firms, whose internal controls worsen compared to the prior SOX year, keep on exhibiting larger abnormal accruals. They state ICD firms that exhibit their ICD can achieve significant improvement in accrual quality. Firms with lasting material weaknesses were not able to improve their accrual quality (cf. ASK et al., 2008, pp. 239-247). These results show that strong internal controls can improve the reliability of financial reporting for accelerated filers (cf. ASK et al., 2008, p. 247).

Singer and You also examined the effects of SOX 404 regarding earnings quality and focused on the reliability and the relevance of earnings. They compare the first relevant two years of SOX 404 (2004-2005) with the two prior years (2002-2003). In contrast to ASK et al. (2008), they use all firms subject to SOX 404 for their sample and a control group including Canadian firms that were not affected by the regulatory intervention in the first two years after the introduction (cf. Singer and You, 2011, pp. 562-565). First, the authors find that the magnitude of absolute abnormal accruals declines significantly for complying firms. The reason may be less manipulative reporting due to the requirements of SOX 404 and thus, earnings reliability seems to be improved. Regarding reporting asymmetry as a proxy for the change in intentional statements, they find evidence that the asymmetry decreases significantly by 15.7 percent from the prior- to post-SOX period. They do not find a significant decrease for their control firms (cf. Singer and You, 2011, pp. 570-571). They find some evidence that SOX 404 has a positive impact on intentional misstatements and hence, reduces them (cf. Singer and You, 2011, p. 577). They conclude that SOX 404 seems to meet the goals, that are improving the reliability and accuracy of corporate disclosure and hence, to protect investors. Complying firms show improved earnings reliability, usefulness and quality after implementation of SOX 404 (cf. Singer and You, 2011, p. 583).

Matching firms' weekly stock returns to the time periods of its reported financial data (1991 to 2005), Hutton, Marcus and Tehranian use the Statement of Cash Flow method aiming to examine the relation between the transparency of financial statements and the distribution of stock price returns. Furthermore, they test whether the SOX and its new requirements and consequences (e.g. regarding penalties for earnings manipulation) has an influence on R^2 of the modified Jones model (cf. Dechow et al., 1995). Latter estimates discretionary accruals and crash risk (cf. Hutton et al., 2009, p. 70). Their tests show that, in contrast to prior-SOX times, the relation between abnormal accruals and idiosyncratic risk almost disappears in post-SOX times. First, this finding suggests that increased scrutiny over accounting practice has an influence on EM. EM seem to disappear in post-SOX times. Second, they show that residuals from the modified Jones model no longer proxy for the opacity of financial reports (cf. Hutton et al., 2009, p. 84).

Rice and Weber use a sample of restating firms and match these restatements to internal control reports between the five periods between the years 2004/2005 and 2008/2009 (cf. Rice and Weber, 2012, p. 819). Overall, they find that approximately two third of the firms with material weaknesses failed to report those on time and therefore, as it is required after the need for a restatement has been announced. A significant decrease, reaching a low of 13.6 percent can be recognized during the last five years of their sample (cf. Rice and Weber, 2012, pp. 825-826). They state that the minority of SOX 404 reportings provide advance warning concerning possible accounting problems. For most firms with a restatement, the ICW that led to those restatements are reported after the disclosure of these restatements. These results provide evidence that the reporting of ICW has been ineffective in practice in some cases and that the decrease in reported material weaknesses is too early as being interpreted as an improvement in internal control practices (cf. Rice and Weber, 2012, p. 837).

Raghunandan and Rama compare prior- and post-SOX audit fees, using a sample containing 660 manufacturing firms complying with SOX 404. They find that the mean audit fees were 86 percent higher than in the fiscal year preceding the SOX. Additionally, audit fees are 43 percent higher for firms with material weakness disclosures compared to those firms without such disclosures. Firms with more business segments need more internal controls. This leads so higher audit fees because the auditor needs to assess the more, and more complex internal controls (cf. Raghunandan and Rama, 2006, pp. 104-108). They find that voluntary disclosures about material weaknesses preceding SOX 404 did not lead to higher audit fees (cf. Raghunandan and Rama, 2006, pp. 110-111). They also find that the cost drivers of the higher audit fees resulted during the post-SOX 404 time. They suggest that a more detailed audit took place in post-SOX time (cf. Raghunandan and Rama, 2006, p. 108). The authors conclude that the SOX led to an extended test of internal controls, and therefore to a change in audit planning – although there have been similar requirements in Auditing Standards before (cf. Raghunandan and Rama, 2006, p. 112).

Hogan and Wilkins compare audit fees of firms prior to an ICD disclosure with audit fees after an ICD disclosure (SOX 404 disclosures excluded), using an audit fee model with an indicator variable that describes firms with ICD disclosures. They compare their results with a sample of firms that do not have ICD disclosures at that time. They find that audit costs increased for ICD firms. When material weaknesses occur, audit fees are much higher. They show that material ICD increase audit fees due to the rising effort of the audit and due to an increase in control risk, too (cf. Hogan and Wilkins, 2008, p. 223-234). Audit fees depend on the type of auditor and the tenure of them. They show differences whether ICD firms hired a Big 4 auditing firm or not. ICD firms that hired such an auditor, have significantly higher audit costs. ICD firms that have hired their auditors for more than two years, they seem to pay significantly lower audit fees that ICD firms that are in the first or second year with an auditor (cf. Hogan and Wilkins, 2008, pp. 229-230).

Bedard and Graham show that there are differences regarding the party that detects ICD. They find that auditors detect about 75 percent of ICD, primarily through control testing, although clients document and test their internal controls, too (cf. Bedard and Graham, 2011, p. 841). Additionally, they find evidence that clients often underestimate ICD severity - but this underestimation declines if the company is well-controlled, which means that there are processes that support SOX 404 requirements (cf. Bedard and Graham, 2011, p. 846). In contrast to SOX 302, SOX 404 seems to have a positive impact on ICD detection because it involves the auditor. Many firms improved their internal controls after ICD have been detected. They criticize the exemption of non-accelerated filers from SOX 404 undermine the aims of SOX. For these firms, there might be a difference concerning perceived and aimed effects (cf. Bedard and Graham, 2011, pp. 851-854).

3.2 Capital Market Consequences

Lambert, Leuz and Verrecchia use a model of multisecurity economy that is consistent with the Capital Asset Pricing Model and shows the expected value and covariance of the future cash flows (cf. Lambert at al., 2007, pp. 389-390). They show that the ratio of this with the sum of all cash flows is a key determinant of the capital cost (cf. Lambert et al., 2007, p. 411) and that there are direct (cf. Lambert et al., 2007, p. 400) and indirect effects of information quality on cost of equity. There is an impact of higher quality information on real decisions on the cash flow value to the investor which influences cost of equity indirectly (cf. Lambert et al., 2007, p. 410).

Francis, LaFond, Olsson and Schipper investigate the relation between the cost of equity capital and seven attributes of earnings which are four accounting-based ones (accrual quality, persistence, predictability and smoothness) and three market-based ones (value relevance, timeliness and conservatism). They find that firms with the least advantageous values of each attribute exhibit larger cost of equity than firms with the most advantageous value (cf. Francis et al., 2004, p. 967-969). Accounting-based attributes, especially "accrual quality", have a larger effect on cost of equity than market-based attributes. Relative to firms with the best accrual quality, firms having the worst accrual quality experience a 371 basis point higher cost of equity. "Persistence" has the second largest impact and "smoothness" has a significant impact on cost of equity (cf. Francis et al., 2004, p. 158). They find evidence that executives' discretionary actions to increase earnings predictability have adverse effects on cost of equity which implies that predictability is not desirable. In contrast, a higher level of predictability than implied by innate determinants increases information risk. Generally, they find evidence that discretionary components depend on management's incentives, opportunities for change and additionally, can be changed more quickly than innate components (cf. Francis et al., 2004, pp. 992-993).

Hammersley et al. (2008) examine the relation between market reaction and the severity of the ICD disclosed under SOX 302. The authors state that especially material weaknesses lead to a significant negative market reaction and the magnitude of ICD is influenced by more severe weaknesses. Control deficiencies and significant deficiencies do not have such a negative impact on the market reaction (cf. Hammersley et al., 2008, p. 158). With multiple regression analyses (cf. Hammersley et al., 2008, p. 159), they show that returns are significantly less negative, although the management stated the absence of ICW and in fact, ICW are present. Returns are weakly less negative if a Big 4 auditing firm is hired. Less auditable ICW affect returns to a higher degree. Regarding the overall effectiveness of SOX 302, the authors conclude that market participants gather more timely information about the quality of firm's internal control system than in prior-SOX-times. To sum it up, the information content of ICD disclosure is affected by the severity of the weakness (cf. Hammersley et al., 2008, pp. 162-164).

ASK, Collins and Kinney use a sample of 326 firms with ICD disclosures made under SOX 302 and reported by SEC. They compare those to 4484 non-disclosing firms in their control sample. Using different proxies (e.g. number of business segments for the complexity) and a logistic regression model (cf. ASK et al., 2007, pp. 177-178), ICD firms seem to have more complex operations, recent organizational changes, greater accounting risk, more auditor resignations and have fewer resources available for internal control. Furthermore, they find that disclosing firms are more likely to be engaged in acquisitions and restructurings, having greater sales growth and a higher level of inventory. Smaller organizations and those that report losses more frequently or being in a financial distress are more likely to report ICD, too. Whenever auditors resign during the prior to disclosures, firms working together with large audit firms, face institutional ownership or having prior restatements, firms are more likely to exhibit ICD. Generally, these two factors seem to have the highest impact on firm's likeliness on disclosing ICD (cf. ASK et al.,

2007, pp. 179-181). Rice and Weber find evidence that firms with financial distresses are less likely to disclose existing ICD under SOX 404. These firms anticipate the behavior of market participants and fear increase of cost of capital. They find evidence that firms are more likely to exhibit ICD when there is a new auditing firm and new executives are present. They add that clients of Big 4 auditing firms are less likely to report ICD due to the ability of the Big 4 firms to "audit around" the internal control issues which leads to a misstatement and therefore have not been relevant for the sample which might have influenced their results. In contrast to ASK et al. (2007), they find larger firms less likely to report their existing ICD due to capital market pressures (cf. Rice and Weber, 2012, pp. 829-831).

ASK, Collins and LaFond compare the change in the cost of equity in times of an unqualified SOX 404 opinion and compare those with previous exhibited ICD under SOX 302 (cf. ASK et al., 2009, pp. 9-10). They find that the cost of equity, both market-adjusted and raw, decrease in average from the 180 days prior to the 180 days after the filing of the unqualified SOX 404 opinion which is consistent with expectations. In case that the independent auditor has an adverse opinion, a modest but insignificant in cost of equity in times of the remediation of the adverse opinion (cf. ASK et al., 2009, pp. 33-34). They find that larger firms with better operating performance, firms that pay dividends more often, and firms with lower volatility of cash flows from operations show lower idiosyncratic risk (cf. ASK et al., 2009, p. 17). Firms with favor characteristics to expect an ICD face a significant decline in cost of equity after the release of an unqualified SOX 404 opinion because investors expected them to have ICD but in fact, no ICD were found. For firms that are not likely to have ICD, no significant change in the cost of equity can be found. They conclude that the SOX 404 opinion provides reward for firms with effective internal controls (cf. ASK et al, 2009, p. 35). Using a sample of 2.515 firms that filed SOX 404 during the period from November 2004 to January 2006 and univariate analysis, Ogneva, Subramanyam, Raghunandan and Rama find evidence that firm size, complexity of operations and financial distress have an influence on cost of capital. They were not able to detect stock price or cost-of-equity effects associated with SOX 404 disclosures after controlling for primitive firm characteristics and analyst forecast bias (cf. Ogneva et al., 2007, pp. 1271-1272).

Using a sample of 330 firms with material weakness disclosures (MWD) under SOX 302, 383 firms disclosing material weaknesses under SOX 404 and a control sample of firms having similar characteristics to firms disclosing material weaknesses but do not exhibit any weaknesses, Beneish, Billings and Hodder compare these samples regarding several factors, for example market reactions and cost of capital (cf. Beneish et al., 2008, pp. 673-674). They find a negative and not transitory market reaction to MWD made under SOX 302 which implies that investors demand for a compensation due to poorer financial reporting quality of the firm they hold. In contrast to that, they do not find a market reaction to SOX 404 disclosures. This finding is not affected by prior disclosures made under SOX 302. This is consistent with the expectation that accelerated filers need to fill SOX 404, usually operate in richer information environments and have significantly better earnings quality. Regarding disclosures made under SOX 302, they find evidence that accelerated filers experience less negative returns than non-accelerated filers. This implies that firms facing higher information-uncertainty before such a disclosure experience stronger negative market reactions. Whenever a Big 4 is involved in the SOX 302 disclosure process, negative market reactions decrease which is consistent with the findings of Hammersley et al. (2008). Afterwards, firms with such a disclosure face abnormally negative forecast revisions and abnormally positive increases in costs of capital, which implies decreasing cash flows and an increase in perceived risk for those firms. In addition, audit and professional fees increase significantly for firms with MWD made under SOX 302 (cf. Beneish et al., 2008, pp. 682 - 685). They do not find such market reactions for firms that make disclosures under SOX 404 which leads to the conclusion that SOX 404 disclosures are not informative. In contrast to that, disclosures under SOX 302 are informative for investors concerning the credibility of firms' financial reporting (cf. Beneish et al., 2008, pp. 690-698).

Li, Pincus and Rego use univariate stock price analysis of marketwide and sample firms' reactions to different SOX-related events, a correlation of sample firms' stock price effects and the extent of firms' EM for different SOX events and additionally, for all events combined (cf. Li et al., 2008, pp. 115-118). In average and regarding several events surrounding the SOX, marketwide and samplewide cumulative abnormal returns are positive. Hence, they find investors having a positive attitude towards the SOX and generally expecting a net positive impact, especially for larger firms. Large firms seem to manage earnings to a higher extent and seem to experience more positive stock returns in post-SOX times than smaller firms. This indicates that investors expect the SOX to improve financial reporting of those firms. Regarding the perceived costs of the SOX, they find investors to expect that the SOX is less costly for larger firms. To conclude, the authors find the SOX provisions and enforcement being more beneficial (cf. Li et al., 2008, pp. 124-128). With a regression analysis, Zhang models the relation between U.S. firm and foreign firm returns (cf. Zhang, 2007, pp. 84-85). Cumulated value- and equal-weighted raw returns are both negative and mostly significant for U.S. and foreign portfolios regarding all key SOX events. This implies that have been other news than SOX at that time, which might reduce explanatory power of her results (cf. Zhang, 2007, pp. 93-94). Additionally, she states that SOX 404 compliance resulted in significant savings for non-accelerated filers which is consistent with the findings of ASK et al. (2009). She finds that many SOX events did not have a significant impact on investors' expectations and results do not support SOX being costly. Regarding one examined coefficient that at least partly shows the extent of shareholder rights, her results cast doubts on the value of the SOX (cf. Zhang, 2007, pp. 108-111).

Using a pool sampled analysis, Cheng, Dhaliwal and Zhang collect data about investment efficiency in the two years following an ICD disclosure under SOX 404 and the year prior to the disclosure. With a regression analysis and a comparison of the results of ICD and non-ICD firms they testes the likelihood of over- and underinvestment (cf. Cheng et al., 2013, pp. 4-5). ICD firms show an increase in real investment efficiency after an ICD disclosure. 78 percent of the ICD firms remedied their ICD which indicates that several changes have been made to increase the quality of internal controls and financial information, and moral hazard has been mitigated. This can be explained with increasing monitoring of shareholders and other stakeholders which leads to a higher quality in financial reporting. To sum it up, they show that the requirements of the SOX have a positive effect on internal control over financial reporting (cf. Cheng et al., 2013, pp. 15-16).

4 Conclusion

The SOX of 2002 aims to improve the credibility of financial information, which is important for investors after facing several frauds. The examined studies show ambiguous results regarding different factors that can be used to evaluate the overall effectiveness of the SOX. Generally, there seem to be differences between the effects of voluntary disclosures under SOX 302, and mandatory disclosures of accelerated filers under SOX 404. Assessing financial reporting and accounting quality, there is evidence that executives keep on managing earnings like before, which casts doubt on the provisions. Other authors find that enhanced scrutiny over accounting practice has a positive impact on EM and mitigates this. Accelerated filers that disclose ICD under SOX 404 seem to increase the reliability of financial statements. Other authors included all SOX 404-complying firms in their studies about the reliability of financial statements and find the SOX being effective. There is evidence that SOX 404 filers generally improved their internal controls after an ICD detection and again, there is criticism regarding the effectiveness for non-accelerated filers due to voluntary characteristics of the provisions. For investors, SOX 404 seems not to provide enough warning in advance regarding present accounting issues. It is mentioned that an extended auditing takes place since the introduction of the SOX 404 which provides benefits regarding the detection of ICD and the reliability of financial statements. Cost of capital seem to be influenced by several other factors (e.g. firm- or auditor-specific ones like firm size or the type of auditor) beside the SOX. Furthermore, the SOX tends to be more beneficial for firms with present effective internal controls. There is evidence that SOX 404 reporting is less informative for investors than SOX 302 reporting due to an already existing, richer information environment of accelerated filers. Therefore, the SOX seems to provide savings for non-accelerated filers due to additional information content available for investors. After an ICD disclosure, firms tend to increase their investment efficiency due to better internal controls. To sum it up, accelerated filers seem to experience more financial accounting and reporting benefits, and non-accelerated filers more cost of capital benefits.

Overall, it seems to be doubtful that the SOX reached its targets to the full extent but some improvements regarding reporting and accounting quality, internal controls and perceived benefits to investors can be recognized. Factors beside the SOX influence these areas, too. Therefore, the SOX is effective to a certain extend. It may be beneficial to revisit some of the early studies in post-SOX times to investigate long-term effects. This literature review includes several factors that help to assess the effectiveness, but there may be more factors. There is a focus on two sections and it may be useful to include the effects of far more sections to draw a conclusion about SOX consequences and its effectiveness. Furthermore, a limited number of studies has been included in this literature review and therefore, an examination of further studies might be useful to see whether the conclusion of this review needs to be revised.

List of References

Ashbaugh-Skaife, H., Collins, D. W., & Kinney, W. R. (2007). The discovery and reporting of internal control deficiencies prior to SOX-mandated audits. Journal of Accounting and Economics, 44, 166-192.

Ashbaugh-Skaife, H., Collins, D. W., Kinney Jr, W. R., & LaFond, R. (2008). The Effect of SOX Internal Control Deficiencies and Their Remediation on Accrual Quality. The Accounting Review, 83(1), 217-250.

Ashbaugh-Skaife, H., Collins, D. W., & LaFond, R. (2009). The Effect of SOX Internal Control Deficiencies on Firm Risk and Cost of Equity. Journal of Accounting Research, 47(1), 1-43.

Bedard, J. C., & Graham, L. (2011). Detection and Severity Classifications of Sarbanes-Oxley Section 404 Internal Control Deficiencies. The Accounting Review, 86(3), 825-855.

Beneish, M. D., Billings, M. B., & Hodder, L. D. (2008). Internal Control Weaknesses and Information Uncertainty. The Accounting Review, 83(3), 665-703.

Cheng, M., Dhaliwal, D., & Zhang, Y. (2013). Does investment efficiency improve after the disclosure of material weaknesses in internal control over financial reporting?. Journal of Accounting and Economics, 56, 1-18.

Cohen, D. A., Dey, A., & Lys, T. Z. (2008). Real and Accrual-based Earnings Management in the Pre-and Post-Sarbanes-Oxley Periods. The accounting review, 83(3), 757-787.

Dechow, P., Sloan, R., & Sweeney, A. (1995). Detecting Earnings Management. The Accounting Review, 70, 193–225.

Dechow, P., Ge, W., & Schrand, C. (2010). Understanding earnings quality: A review of the proxies, their determinants and their consequences. Journal of Accounting and Economics, 50, 344-401.

DeFond, M. L., & Francis, J. R. (2005). Audit Research after Sarbanes-Oxley. Auditing: A Journal of Practice & Theory, 24(s-1), 5-30.

DeFond, M.L., & Zhang, J. (2014). A review of archival auditing research. Journal of Accounting and Economics, 58, 275-326.

Francis, J., LaFond, R., Olsson, P. M., & Schipper, K. (2004). Costs of Equity and Earnings Attributes. The Accounting Review, 79(4), 967-1010.

Hammersley, J. S., Myers, L. A., & Shakespeare, C. (2008). Market reactions to the disclosure of internal control weaknesses and to the characteristics of those weaknesses under section 302 of the Sarbanes Oxley Act of 2002. Review of Accounting Studies, 13, 141-165.

Hausman, J. A. (1978). Specification Tests in Econometrics. Econometrica, 46 (6), 1251–1271.

Hogan, C. E., & Wilkins, M. S. (2008). Evidence on the Audit Risk Model: Do Auditors Increase Audit Fees in the Presence of Internal Control Deficiencies?. Contemporary Accounting Research, 25(1), 219-242.

Hutton, A. P., Marcus, A. J., & Tehranian, H. (2009). Opaque financial reports, R^2, and crash risk. Journal of Financial Economics, 94, 67-86.

Jones, J. J. (1991). Earnings Management During Import Relief Investigations. Journal of accounting research, 29(2), 193-228.

Lambert, R., Leuz, C., & Verrecchia, R. E. (2007). Accounting Information, Disclosure, and the Cost of Capital. Journal of Accounting Research, 45(2), 385-420.

Leuz, C., & Wysocki, P. D. (2016). The Economics of Disclosure and Financial Reporting Regulation: Evidence and Suggestions for Future Research. Journal of Accounting Research, 54(2), 525-622.

Li, H., Pincus, M., & Rego, S. O. (2008). Market Reaction to Events Surrounding the Sarbanes-Oxley Act of 2002 and Earnings Management. The Journal of Law and Economics, 51(1), 111-134.

Ogneva, M., Subramanyam, K. R., & Raghunandan and Rama, K. (2007). Internal Control Weakness and Cost of Equity: Evidence from SOX Section 404 Disclosures. The Accounting Review, 82(5), 1255-1297.

Public Company Accounting Oversight Board (2004). Auditing Standard No. 2. An Audit of Internal Control Over Financial Reporting Performed in Conjunction With an Audit of Financial Statements. Washington, DC: PCAOB.

Raghunandan, K., & Rama, D. V. (2006). SOX Section 404 Material Weakness Disclosures and Audit Fees. Auditing: A Journal of Practice & Theory, 25(1), 99-114.

Rice, S. C., & Weber, D. P. (2012). How Effective Is Internal Control Reporting under SOX 404? Determinants of the (Non-) Disclosure of Existing Material Weaknesses. Journal of Accounting Research, 50(3), 811-843.

Romano, R. (2005). The Sarbanes-Oxley Act and the Making of Quack Corporate Governance. The Yale Law Journal, 114(7), 1521-1611.

Roychowdhury, S. (2006). Earnings management through real activities manipulation. Journal of Accounting and Economics, 42, 335-370.

Sarbanes–Oxley Act (2002): Pub.L. 107–204, 116 Stat. 745, enacted July 30, 2002.

Singer, Z., & You, H. (2011). The Effect of Section 404 of the Sarbanes-Oxley Act on Earnings Quality. Journal of Accounting, Auditing & Finance, 26(3), 556-589.

Zang, A. Y. (2012). Evidence on the Trade-Off between Real Activities Manipulation and Accrual-Based Earnings Management. The Accounting Review, 87(2), 675-703.

Zhang, I. X. (2007). Economic Consequences of the Sarbanes–Oxley Act of 2002. Journal of Accounting and Economics, 44, 74-115.

YOUR KNOWLEDGE HAS VALUE

- We will publish your bachelor's and master's thesis, essays and papers

- Your own eBook and book - sold worldwide in all relevant shops

- Earn money with each sale

Upload your text at www.GRIN.com
and publish for free